Race
Around the
Kingdom

A play by Jill McDougall

Illustrations by Amy Lane

Race Around the Kingdom

Text: Jill McDougall
Publishers: Tania Mazzeo and Eliza Webb
Series consultant: Amanda Sutera
  Hands on Heads Consulting
Editor: Gemma Smith
Project editor: Annabel Smith
Designer: Jess Kelly
Project designer: Danielle Maccarone
Illustrations: Amy Lane
Production controller: Renee Tome

NovaStar

ISBN 978 0 17 033424 2

Cengage Learning Australia
Level 5, 80 Dorcas Street
Southbank VIC 3006 Australia
Phone: 1300 790 853
Email: aust.nelsonprimary@cengage.com

For learning solutions, visit **cengage.com.au**

Printed in China by 1010 Printing International Ltd
1 2 3 4 5 6 7 28 27 26 25 24

*Nelson acknowledges the Traditional Owners and Custodians
of the lands of all First Nations Peoples. We pay respect
to Elders past and present, and extend that respect to
all First Nations Peoples today.*

People in the Play

Gretel

Prince Charming

Hansel

Rapunzel

Sleeping Beauty

Cinderella

Narrator

Narrator *(talking quietly)*
We are in a TV studio and the show is about to start. The hosts, Hansel and Gretel, are standing by. *Shhh.*

Gretel *(holding microphone)*
Good evening to everyone across the fairy tale kingdom. Welcome to your favourite reality show, *Race Around the Kingdom*. Tonight's contestant is a real-life fairy tale prince. It's the one ... the only ... *Prince Charming*!

(The audience claps.)

Prince Charming
Oh ... um, thank you.

Gretel *(to Hansel)*
Can you tell us more about our princely contestant, Hansel?

Hansel *(holding microphone)*
Yes, Gretel. Prince Charming is a big fan of the latest fashion for fairy tale princes. As you can see, his favourite look right now is puffy sleeves, tight pants and extra-shiny boots.

Prince Charming

Actually, your wardrobe department made me wear this silly outfit. My *real* passion is cooking, and I usually potter about the palace kitchen in my tracksuit pants.

Gretel

Ha ha! Our contestant has a *charming* sense of humour. So are you ready to play, Prince?

Prince Charming

Play? What? Er, well, you see, I don't –

Gretel *(interrupting)*

Prince Charming, you'll race against the clock to complete three challenges before your time runs out.

Hansel

And here's your first challenge. You'll proceed to the middle of a thick forest, where you'll locate a tower.

Prince Charming

Wait a minute! Forest? Tower? I'm in the wrong reality TV show! I thought this was *The Kingdom's Most Amazing Chef.*

Gretel

What a comedian! Please continue, Hansel.

Hansel

At the top of the tower, there's a damsel in distress, named Rapunzel. You, Prince Charming, must rescue her from the tower.

Prince Charming

Are you serious? I've never even rescued a kitten. Not even a small one!

Gretel *(looking at her watch)*
And your time starts ... now!

Narrator

Without further ado, the prince hurries towards a thick forest with spiky bushes and tangly vines.

Prince Charming *(panting)*

This forest is thick with spiky bushes and the vines are extremely tangly. They're stuck all over my puffy sleeves and tight pants.

Rapunzel *(calling out)*

Hey, you! Hurry up!

Prince Charming *(looking up)*

Hello up there! I'm Prince Charming, and you must be Rapunzel. I recognise you by your extra-long hair.

Rapunzel

Quit the small talk, Prince, and get me down from here! My phone is running out of battery.

Prince Charming

No problem. Um … do you see an extension ladder anywhere?

Rapunzel

What sort of prince are you anyway? Throw up some of those tangly vines.

Narrator

Prince Charming tosses up some tangly vines, and, in the blink of an eye, Rapunzel has made them into a ladder and climbed down.

(The audience claps.)

Hansel *(from the studio couch)*
Congratulations, Prince Charming. You have rescued your first damsel in distress.

Rapunzel
Get real, dude! I rescued myself.

Prince Charming

That's true, Hansel. Rapunzel here did a seriously awesome job of rescuing herself. So, what happens now?

Hansel

You have two more damsels to rescue before your time runs out. If you succeed, you'll win ...

Gretel *(in an excited voice)*

... an amazing saucepan set with see-through lids!

Prince Charming

That sounds cool. Who's the next damsel, Mr High Pants?

Hansel

My name is Hansel! I can't help it if the wardrobe department dressed me in this wacky outfit.

Gretel

Stop complaining! I have to wear a silly white apron and tippy-tappy shoes!

Prince Charming

Can we please get back to the damsels? I want my saucepan set.

Hansel

Of course, Prince Charming. The next damsel to be rescued is called Sleeping Beauty. She's been asleep for a long time, and your challenge is simple. You must wake her up.

Rapunzel

I know exactly where that annoying girl is. Her noisy snores have been keeping me awake for years!

Narrator

Rapunzel leads Prince Charming to a smallish castle, and, sure enough, there on the couch lies Sleeping Beauty, snoring loudly.

Sleeping Beauty

Snore! Snore!

Prince Charming *(loudly)*

Hey, sleepyhead! Wake up!

Sleeping Beauty

Snort!

Prince Charming
I'll tickle her toes. That never fails to
wake the queen up.

Tickle, tickle, tickle.

Sleeping Beauty *(sleepily)*
Snort!

Prince Charming

I'll pour this cold water down her neck.
That never fails to wake the king up.

Narrator

Prince Charming pours a glassful of water
over Sleeping Beauty.

Sleeping Beauty *(loudly)*

Snort!

Rapunzel

I have an idea. I'll set the alarm on my
phone and turn up the volume.

Two seconds ... one second ...

Narrator

Suddenly, the room is filled with a terrible
sound: *skwee brumm brumm skooooooo.*

Sleeping Beauty *(jumping up)*

Argh! Where am I? What's going on?
And what is that awful noise?

Rapunzel

It's a garbage truck! It's my favourite wake-up sound.

Prince Charming *(proudly)*

We used it to rescue you from your long sleep. Well done us!

Which damsel is next, Mr High ... Hansel?

Hansel *(from the studio couch)*

Your final challenge is to locate a damsel called Cinderella, who always runs away from the ball.

Sleeping Beauty

Why? Is she a netball player?

Prince Charming

Er ... probably not, Sleeping Beauty.
You see, a ball is a place where –

Sleeping Beauty

Ahem ... I was
making a joke,
Your Royal
Prince-ness.
I say, I hope
they have some
food at this ball.
I feel like I haven't
eaten for a hundred years.

Rapunzel

Actually, you haven't. Come on, let's all
go together.

Narrator

Prince Charming, Rapunzel and Sleeping
Beauty link arms and set off for the ball.

Sleeping Beauty

Here we are, and there's the food table!
Come on, Rappie. Let's go and demolish
some pizza!

Prince Charming

I see a damsel in glass slippers. I bet
that's Cinderella.

(He walks over.)

Hello, dear damsel. Would you like to dance?

Cinderella

No way! I've been wearing these silly glass
slippers all night, and I've got blisters the
size of Jupiter.

Prince Charming *(puzzled)*

Who is this "Jupiter"? Is he here to rescue you too?

Narrator

Before Cinderella can answer, the clock strikes midnight.

Cinderella

That's my cue! I have to leave the ball before my golden coach turns into a rather large vegetable.

Narrator

But alas, it's too late. Sitting outside the ballroom is an enormous orange pumpkin.

Rapunzel

How dreadful! You won't get far in that!

Sleeping Beauty *(eating hungrily)*

It's a tragedy. But I say, this cake is yum!

Cinderella *(pointing to the pumpkin)*

What am I to do with this ... monstrosity?

Prince Charming

I know exactly what to do with it. Help me roll it to the palace kitchen. It will make the perfect pumpkin soup!

Gretel

And you can use your new saucepan set with the see-through lids! You've completed all three challenges in record time. Congratulations!

(The audience claps.)

Narrator

In no time at all, Prince Charming is dishing out ladles of hot soup for his new friends. Everyone agrees it's the best soup ever.

Gretel

Ladies and gentlemen and everyone else, this brings us to the end of this series of *Race Around the Kingdom*.

Hansel

Be sure to watch next week for our new reality TV show – *The Kingdom's Most Amazing Chef*.

Prince Charming *(winking at audience)*
You might even see a familiar face!

(The audience claps loudly.)